Slipping into another world

Bhuwan Thapaliya

Ukiyoto Publishing

All global publishing rights are held by

Ukiyoto Publishing

Published in 2025

Content Copyright © Bhuwan Thapaliya
ISBN 9789367950166

*All rights reserved.
No part of this publication may be reproduced,
transmitted, or stored in a retrieval system, in any
form by any means, electronic, mechanical,
photocopying, recording or otherwise, without the
prior permission of the publisher.*

The moral rights of the author have been asserted.

*This book is sold subject to the condition that it shall
not by way of trade or otherwise, be lent, resold, hired
out or otherwise circulated, without the publisher's
prior consent, in any form of binding or cover other
than that in which it is published.*

www.ukiyoto.com

I extend my heartfelt respect and deep appreciation to everyone who has supported me on my journey as a poet. I am profoundly indebted to those who have placed their faith in my abilities and embraced my work with open hearts. Your encouragement and belief have been the foundation upon which I continue to build my art, inspiring me to weave emotions into words and bring my thoughts to life. It is your unwavering support that fuels my creative spirit, and for that, I am eternally grateful.

Contents

A dead cell phone	1
Slipping into another world	3
Navel	5
Ginger tea	6
Sunny august afternoon in Covid	8
Buddha and me	11
Marching Millions	13
Within	15
How a poem begins?	17
Reading a poem to my father	19
Trudging up	23
Addiction	25
Fate	27
Lily in my hand	28
Only to meet Yuyu	30
My poem	34
Himalayan Jazz Bar	36
My father's old coat	39
Deep in Dolpo	42
Grandma	44
A Mountain Pass	46
Last flight	49
Stains	52
About the Author	*53*

A dead cell phone

Her late grandfather came with a hobbling gait
in her dream last night. They were in a tented camp
on the river bank, nearby their abandoned farmhouse.
He poured a large peg of Khukri Rum, drank it
with a sly smile and sat down beside her
on a wobbly camp cot, lit a cigarette,
nostalgic smoke curled into the night.
He took a sip again and through a ragged crack
glimpsed outside and beamed at a star worm crawling
among the fallen leaves, and thereafter listened for hours and hours,
the melody of those olden times. Its lyrics now hidden, buried,
awaiting discovery as a child with several siblings,
all forgotten, overlooked, lost.
The sky roared and the wind blew hard.
"I think I have to go now," he whispered in her ear.
"So where do you go from here, grand pa," she asked.
"I will continue to travel
but now it is all about reverse travel.
I will move to a place where I'd been before

and stay maybe a week, a month , a year,
and completely alter the way I see the future.
I see my father. I see my mother.
I see your grandmother. I see you,"
he answered her with a somber smile
and requested her to stay connected with her past.
She nodded her head and said I will grandpa.
Next morning, she woke up late
to a dead cell phone
beside her bed in a wooden rack.
No charger in sight.

Slipping into another world

A fragrance of serenity
erupting from assorted flowers
in the wilderness of her smiles
moisturizes my emotions
and takes me far away,
very far away from a landscape
which has familiar elements
to a place where there is
no conflict between
human proportions
and the proportions
of the discarded
manmade objects.
The surge of her smiles
has transformed
my mind
in many ways.
I feel I am slipping
into another world.
A world

4 Slipping into another world

where the heart
of the democracy
isn't cracked open,
parched
and sun-dried.
A world
far away from
blaring horns
and choking fumes
of their
vociferous thoughts.

Navel

The sun has risen
from her navel.
An inked snake
twists around her waist,
and the scorpion crawls
 up her emaciated torso.
Moist are her eyes.
And a beautiful
rainbow
dangles
over her breasts.
Nature encompasses all.
The world is madly in love again.
While the sun
took its time
to caress the sky
I sat there beside her
with a drink
looking at her
without winking my eyes.

Ginger tea

I am sitting by the window now,
and there is nothing to hinder
my irrational thoughts
from wondering as much as I please.
Life laughs at me, of course,
but one expects that in jealousy.
I may spend all my afternoon
looking outside
though I am not interested
in such a time- prone,
statistics- aware society,
or I could simply pull dad's
stuff out of a storage box
and bask them in the sun.
Dad's favorite coffee glass
may come out again first.
But I have a feeling that
from now on I'd be having
ginger tea, not coffee.
The next few days,

I'm going swimming.
I will plunge into the
bottomless chasm
of my memories
and drown
my fathers
favorite coffee glass.
Let me rejoice,

my renaissance.

Sunny August afternoon in Covid

On a sunny August afternoon
in Kathmandu, I heard the whine of sirens.
Looking up from my laptop screen,
I saw ambulances careering up
the punctured streets
as the wounded city
continues to show
the ravages of its lost dreams
muffled by the canopy
of the uncertainties.
Broken limbs of hope
were all over the streets.
The scale of financial strain,
gigantic.
Despair, in some ways,
had just begun.
I slowly lowered by head
and closed my eyes.
The air above me was thick

with the spirit of the living dead.
"This is between you and me,"
my spirit said in a hushed voice suddenly.
The virus is ruthless but it will go away soon.
Don't let it erode your core.
I opened my eyes and gradually
stood up from my chair
and in the distance I saw
a skinny chameleon
scratching itself in the Sun.
And nearby squirrels
were pampering themselves
on the branches of a guava tree.
They say time heals
a lot of wounds, a lot of wounds.
This time, it's going to be difficult.
There are deep, systemic things
that we need to fix.
Time can't fix it for us
and it never will.
Our future may hinge
on our ability
to heal the wounds ourselves

and don't depend upon the time
to heal it for us, always.

Buddha and me

We looked at each other
in disbelief.
Buddha
and me.
He was clad
in an age old
duplicate polo sweatshirt
and a hippie donated blue jeans.

Whereas I was
wearing a saffron robe .
After a while,
little rattled
by our silence,
we smiled indulgently
and then looked at each other
with belief.
The blue of the sky
beckoned invitingly.
We sat together

Slipping into another world

dipping out feet
in the creek
within a circle of ferns
and mature tall trees
far from the horns
and screeching brakes
of time.

Marching Millions

Every moment
the pandemic slashes us
into pieces,
pauses our heart
as the scruffiness
of industrial graveyards
against which trodden grass
and plants strive to survive.
However, we manage to
sew ourselves somehow and wonder,
when and how we would reclaim a normal life.
Anger mounts, patience wears thin.
Moths lit up our sky, our stars are very dim.
We are in the shadows; the virus is making
mockery of our misery, pandemic stinks.
We are the marching millions.
Our journey never ends.
The more we march towards hope
the more our hope moves
further away from us.

Eyes closed and hands together in prayer
we bow our heads to the ground.
Our prayers may not be audible enough
to carry messages of a people's faith
to the gods themselves.
We have become
as insignificant as motifs
on a mud wall.
The rhetoric of normality
goes far beyond us.

Within

"We've to travel; travel far and wide
to understand the essences of the world,"
he whispered with an arid smile.
"But what about the world within us,
where there are innumerable
elements to experience,"
she countered in a silken voice,
and wiggled her eyes
in a bedroom with sweeping view
of the sacred hills.
Yes, yes, yes, he stammered, smiled
and lifted her high in the air.
Their lips opened up as an umbrella.
They rested for a while beneath it,
inhaling deep sap of the salubrious wind,
 then caressed each other,
word by word, line by line,
rhyme by rhyme as a poet, and sat together
 watching the snow tipped peaks
of their dreams across the horizon

without winking their animated eyes.
Their hands as their faith
stacked one atop the other.

How a poem begins?

Whenever I sit down to write,
they always run into each other
and fight like stray dogs
in the weary backstreets
of the bustling metropolis.
My heart and my mind.
I smoke one cigarette
after another,
puffing furiously along
until a sequence of photographs
of my ancestors in motion
passes before my eyes
or until the sun smiles
on the fecund grassland
of my emotions
and thoughts
stomp around
in huge herds.
Then I start to write
inhaling muffled smell

of an empty page.
My words crumble,
they encircle me
then tear me apart
and disappear
blinking in the dark.
A ray of light
spins in the darkness.
A poem slowly grows
with it and without.
A beautiful
imperfectly perfect
creation.
Its lips open up.
I drink expresso
from a cup
of its mouth.
A holy bridge.

Reading a poem to my father

One evening
to ward off the inertia
stemming out of
current pandemic
I read aloud to my father,
one of my favorite poems
from Yuyutsu Sharma's
The Lake Fewa and a Horse.
A high blood pressure
and a chronic diabetics patient,
though he can
read only the headlines
of a newspaper,
his glare can be as rigid
as a row of commas
on a page of my poems;
he can hush us all
by just clearing his throat.

There is nothing lyrical about him.
His emotions are packed full

as the groceries on the supermarket shelves.
Often it's not easy to recite poems
in front of him and my reading
that lonely evening was scratchy
as I was shaking from it.

Sensing my anxiety,
he grabbed the book
from my hands
and lifting it to his eyes
to discover Yuyu's affair
with the Himalayas.
After industriously reading a few poems,
I noticed a flame of joy liven up
his dark silvery eyes.

He nodded his head and smiled,
"Oh yes, this I remember,
and this too, how we washed
our clothes in the river,
and cooked on an open fire.
We had straw mats instead
of dining tables and for brunch
we often had beaten rice flakes and curd,

and families gathered before the fire
united before the sunlight left us
for a long cold night."

As the day's last thumping kiss
painted the sky,
my father perched on the side
of the antique sofa,
smiled. 'I feel as if Yuyu's poems
has unfastened my past.
His verses have struck
in me a trumpet of triumph,
a yearning to return and
sweet smell the soil from which I've sprung .

Son, I can feel it.
His poems have triggered
the sensations of hope in my aging heart.
They've fed me with a gusto
to smile evermore.

I wish I could read
this book on and on
but my eyes won't permit.

I have one request:
Would you call Yuyu
and ask him to come out with
a recording of his poems for his readers like me.

I was ecstatic–
a happy, hopeful father!
Can there be anything more lyrical
than a father's smile streaming all over our horizons?

The line was drawn that day,
a turning point ensuing
my father's newfound health.

For making my father smile
and sprouting in our
Kathmandu courtyard
the hidden seeds of his long
forgotten hillside paths.
I salute you poet, I salute you!

Trudging up

Forlorn in the lethal frozen slopes
just a few meters beneath
the summit of my dreams
I bowed down with exhaustion,
in a cold, gritty wind.
Exhausted, with hope-tipped
mountaineering sticks in hands,
I wondered about my ancestor's life
behind the blue door of the sky cabinets
and saw clothes of my ancestors fluttering
on a half broken clotheslines in the sky.
My vision slowly distorted,
an attitude sickness
or maybe more.
I coughed thrice, and suddenly
the spirit of my long lost dreams
in the canyons of the realism

rose from their siesta and danced
around me shouting brisk words

of encouragement.
"Don't give up, it's only
 a mere altitude headache
you will get over it,"
they kept on chanting.
I stood shakily
and found myself
trudging up
my dreams
gravelly trails
once again.

Addiction

He comes home
late in the evening
only to slump in front
of the television,
often with
an alcoholic drink.
Her response
was always the same:
turn the television off,
curse him aloud,
then head to the bedroom
and slam the door behind.
Next morning they wake up
and look at each other
in disbelief
with shaggy thoughts
and go out to the lawn
through the large glass door
of the living room,
into the brilliance

of the mid-morning sunshine,
with a cup of black coffee
in their hands
and sit down
in the wobbly chair.
With the zephyr
coming in,
and birds calling,
they feel no hurry
to get back to
anything at all,
and watch
their future dance
in sheer abandon,
its locks
falling in disarray
on fates broad shoulder
as wild orchids
that hang out of trees.

Fate

Like a wounded bird
in the iron cage,
half dead as in a trance.
Such is our story today,
grappling in rage
with our ordained fate.
Those smiles,
those covid smiles
changed entirely
the way we perceive
our future
and extol our past.
Our hope begins to tremble.
Our dreams begin to sway.
Is it the beginning of the end
of mankind's reign on earth?
We don't know. We really don't know.
We may, as a species, pass on too.
The earth keeps finding something new.

Lily in my hand

I love the forest,
little creeks and ferns
and singing birds.
There is not a tree
that I cannot talk to.
There is not a bird
that I cannot chirp to.
I often go deep
inside the woods
and take a long nap
using my bag as a pillow
listening to her
billowing sighs,
remote from the
screeching bulldozers
and admire the ferns
that inhabited
the earth
long before
flowering plants.

A colourful lily
often seduces me
from a shady place
in the distance
and I go further deep
inside the woods
and see
tiny droplets
of my ancestors
hanging from
its petals.
Then come back
with a lily in my hand.

Only to meet Yuyu

(A Poem in pandemic for my mentor, Mr. Yuyutsu Sharma)

There's no one to talk to
in the buzzing streets of Kathmandu,
everything has frozen in this town;
no calm even in the mannequin eyes standing
erect in the fancy boutiques along
the termite eaten streets of the city.

Swirling dust and choking fumes infuse
with the breath of pallid roadside trees.
The landscape changes as the rain falls
and the leaves smile again.
Isolated raindrops, expelled lovers
before their first kiss lie
along the twigs of the branches
 — round, sparkling globules
— undulating without descent.

And then everything changes again
when the leaves falls, everything changes.
Once they touch the ground

they turn into ciphers
the sublime truths of life
beneath their layers.

The barriers people create between nature
and windows, walls, doors,
are not really barriers in Kathmandu
for you can talk with all. And you can
never be bored, you just have to sit
and look at the people passing by
and there's so much to say.

Gazing deep into Buddha's serpent eyes,
one feels like being in a Time Machine.
But sometimes, there is silence,
utter silence of a sadhu's stare
into the infinity in Kathmandu,
silence of old mansions
where only a caretaker kills time.
And the civilians of the nation disappear
like the water sprouts of the valley
choking my soul to the core .

There is not a person that I can talk to
in the rustic streets of Kathmandu.

32   Slipping into another world

I am as forlorn and lonely as a man snoozing
on an unused railway tracks
in some old Indian town.

I hardly ever go out now.
I am fed up with the squalor of urban life
where everyone is not what they seem to be.
I should have stayed back
at the banks of the river Sunkoshi
that festoons my village
chewing the pebbles
of my pristine dreams.

These days, I leave my home
only to meet Yuyu, chat up nonstop over
endless cups of masala tea
at Shreejana's While Lotus Book Shop,
watching the poems turn into
colorful serpents and climb the murky trees
enveloped in grey mist.

I leave my home only to meet Yuyu
and share a joke or two,
listen to his sharp one liners.
anecdotes of his travels from

the shores of his dreams
and laugh aloud
celebrating full- blooded flame
lighted in honor of his vagabond Muse.

His words little by little entrap you,
enwrap your soul in their singing silence,
at the end of the day feeding my shriveled soul.

And often as we wave goodbye,
he delves deep into a silent
that soon turns into a river of endless vigor.

Poem dangles from
the edge of his serene mouth.

And a dreamy prose
dances over his misty eyelashes.

And the silence
an ode to the Kathmandu Valley.
If one dare to pay heed.

My poem

My poem could develop
from roadside flowers and trees
or from a face on the street,
and also from an exquisite
Persian carpet mounted
on the wooden floor
or from a pastoral folk song.
It could develop
from vine maples
dressed in autumn hues
or from an Aboriginal painting
from Perth.
It could develop
from a low Italian lamp
and Belgian rug,
or from wall mounted
intricate brass mirrors.
It could develop
from Nepalese thangkas
or from a stunning Buddha

in gold leaf reclining on the altar table .
It could develop while mixing a salad,
or dabbling in my favorite Italian cuisine
or having a black tea
and a hard-boiled egg in the morning.
It could also erupt from anywhere,
my grey beard and taper into
a square nook between tall plants

Himalayan Jazz Bar

The Sun has risen
but it is not yet warm enough
to come out in the open and dance.
Nonetheless wherever they are,
they feel pretty euphoric and warm.
Now at least they can listen
to their special songs and smile.
Let them hold
their hands for a while
in the corner of their favorite jazz bar
perched up on a hillock, a rambling
garden all around, extended with
glorious trees, garlanded by
vibrant climbers atop
and fancy swaying shrubs below.
Sweet zephyr encompasses all.
The majestic Himalayas
smiles in the distance
through a window
between the sturdy trees.

Let the fragrance of the
soothing jazz music
mellow furthermore
with their sensual midday sighs.

Let them gaze into their eyes
and dream of harmony,
of peace and liberty,
which we, in our madness
have separated,
and have devised a realism
that is absurd, and pretend to
find solace in a bolt
of the lightning .
A young guitarist
finds himself looking out
at the snow tipped mountains
across the horizon
and soaking in
all the atmosphere,
then delves further
into the elusive
melodies of the Jazz
conveying a wholly aesthetic

mood of infectious joyousness .
The sunlight filters
through his guitar strings
and the melody
of the monsoon flood water
that run off steep hillsides
through wild shrubbery,
animated with bird songs
seduces all.
O what a sight to behold.

My father's old coat

Dust on my father's old coat
dances as thoughts
on a frying pan
and his tattered hope
as his clothes flutter forlorn
on a half-broken clothesline.

He is down
and almost out, in Kathmandu.
Yet he prowls, he prowls evermore,
through the streets
looking for his fate
in the pothole paths of the city,
trodden by the twisted neck
of the continuous misfortune
where men are snaring
the faith of men
in the altar of
the sunken whore's destitute.

Back then, the hills
around his heart were thickly wooded
but now, the wild trees have gone.
Deforestation of hope,
and the drought of dreams
have formed a vicious circle -
now the hills are all barren brown.

Yet the old man prowls
on and on.
And often on hands and knees,

he scours the ground
collecting every fossil
of his elapsed smiles.
Purely nostalgic, whimsy,
or a maggot munching
a Pipal leaf? No one knows.

I often watch him
breast the wave
with cerulean thoughts
in my head.
He looks jaded,

but in the city of his eyes
there are poems within poems.

I've read pretty much
everything
I could lay my eyes on.
The verses in his eyes
play themselves out
before my eyes
as a writer's bad dream
– ritualistic slaughter
of language and vocabularies.

Deep in Dolpo

Deep in Dolpo*, a blue-eyed Buddhist monk
sank so deep into prayers inside a historic monastery
that his breathing became an annoyance to him.
Around him, the crumbling mural deities,
deities that counter sickness, intruders, and evil,
smiled and snarled. Outside, the hazy sun tinted
on Mount Dhaulagiri's bald head

with furrowed forehead cracks, and stomach,
too shallow, devoid of snow.
A golden eagle flew across the serene sky.
It flew back and forth, rose, and fell
as The Dow Jones Industrial Average.
And a weathered prayer flag mounted
on a sturdy wooden pole outside
the monastery driven into a heap of stones
howled as the fearsome goddess Kali
in the holy mountain wind.
After an hour or so,
the monk stood up and watched

the blazing sun intensely from the corner of his eyes
leaning against his trodden hope.

"As a child, I never imagined that one day
I would see the Mountain devoid of snow
and I don't know when will I see
the musk deer and the snow leopard again,"
he whispered to himself and sauntered
without any purpose behind the caravan of yaks,
the divine mountain troupe, walking together
at their pace carrying supplies and goods.
When the twilight settled in, he walked barefoot
with his eyes on the setting sun, entirely mesmerized,
as if he'd noticed the sunset for the first time.
He wanted to embrace it and kiss it hard
but he could not stop it from dipping down.

Dolpo is a high-altitude culturally Tibetan region in the upper part of the Dolpa District of western Nepal.

Grandma

She rose from her makeshift rustic bed
and strained her eyes in the morning sun
shining through termite eaten windows.
Drank a glass of basil water and then made
her way up a trail on a tough terrain
 to the forest overlooking the Sunkoshi River
 to collect fodder for her cattle.
An old kerosene lamp hangs in the window
of an abandoned building and carved wooden deities
flank a rickety gate. Poor eyesight, back permanently bent
from the burden of heavy loads, feet deformed
and ravaged by walking barefoot on rough terrain,
she looked older than her ancestral deity on a hilltop nearby.
Dry corn leaves rustled underfoot. She picked one

and rubbed it in her palms, smiling at herself
and kneeled down to quench her thirst from a
little burbling creek neighboring her path.
Thereafter, she hastened her pace humming

her favorite song, sung by her mother
when she was young.
"Plant a tree, then another, then many more.
Maybe we will be able to cleanse the world."
Every time when she hums this song,
she feels her mother humming it with her too.
Whistling, she walked deep inside the forest
and soon her doko was fully fodder crammed.
She looked at the deep blue sky and grinned
as a little girl with rhododendron flowers
in her hands high up in the Himalayas
and then sauntered slowly down the hill,
carrying heavy doko on her back with the namlo straps
on her forehead smiling at her neighbors
showing her uneven teeth, as they prepare
to spread animal fertilizer on their fields.
On the back of her polka-dotted cow,

there was a little bird.
The cows mooed loudly after seeing her.
She fed the cattle and then went inside the kitchen
to cook dal, bhat and tarkari.
In the adjoining room, her hungry children were
already getting ready for their school.

A Mountain Pass

(In memory of Joe Pass)

A woman sits in a window frame
of old carved birds, listening to her
grandson in his jeans playing fig leaf music
in her home in Koshidekha,
a village in Nepal.
His music reminded her
of those lovely spring evenings
hopping the jazz clubs in New Orleans
with her late husband,
a Jazz fan like her,
and a handsome Air Force pilot
with short hair who was killed
by friendly fire in the Gulf War.
She was nostalgic the whole day,
and that evening, she lit an incense stick
with a lighter and sat beneath
the picture of her husband
in the living room and
conversed with his soul.

When she opened her eyes,
Joe Pass was there with his
Gibson ES-175 guitar in his hands.
"Don't be surprised. Lead me to a place
where I can play for you," Joe said.
She was stunned but she said nothing
and then Joe smiled.
She smiled back,
and they stepped through
a narrow door
into the open room
where an enormous mural
depicted a Buddha
who sat cross-legged
atop a cloud
holding a conch shell in one hand
and a silver bowl in the other
ignited the room.
Joe smiled again and began to play
his legendary tunes.
She sobbed and coughed
and then got herself a glass of water
and then stood leaning in the window,
her back to the room, gazing out.

Through the window in the moonlight,
she saw a man with short grey hair
turn his prayer wheel as a Buddhist monk,
humming and vanishing
beneath the big banyan tree.
She turned around in excitement
but Joe was not there.
Nearby, the wooden bridge
swayed and creaked,
and a brook burbled
through a mountain pass.

Last flight

She waited for him
at the dinner table

long after
the dinner time
had passed.

She'd been
fooled by him.

He took
the last flight

beyond
the blue sky

and never
came back.

High cheek bones

and with quaky eyes,

she is
waiting for him,

holding
a cup of masala memories.

Clotheslines hang about
 in the darkness
and there is light
only in his room.

His cupboards
 all open

a stack of folded,
crumpled clothes

waiting
to be ironed

gives
a convivial look..

The dustbin
in his room

empty.

It has kept
its secrets.

A housefly buzzed
around the room

and then sat on the side
of his picture frame

on the wall.

She reached out
and chased it away

out of the room.

Stains

Such are the stains of my kisses
in the air – sensual, lucid and warm.
And as a sturdy mountain goat, with a
bell hung on its neck, my lips hovers
above the atmosphere's throat
reeking a soft and solemn – respire of love.
And O' hapless song birds, children of
the goddess Saraswati, listen to my songs,
floating over the Himalayas, as the first
quaff of the dawn, that tumbles down
the snowy peaks and unleashes us all
from the dreadful cough and cold.

About the Author

Bhuwan Thapaliya

Bhuwan Thapaliya is a distinguished poet from Kathmandu, Nepal, who blends his professional life as an economist with his passion for poetry. He has authored four poetry collections, including Safa Tempo (published by Nirala, New Delhi). His work has garnered international acclaim, appearing in renowned journals and being featured in numerous global anthologies. These include Life in Quarantine: Witnessing Global Pandemic Initiative—a project supported by the Poetic Media Lab and the Center for Spatial and Textual Analysis at Stanford University—along with initiatives like the International Human Rights Art Festival and Poetry and Covid, which was funded by the UK Arts and Humanities Research Council in collaboration with the University of Plymouth and Nottingham Trent University.

Thapaliya's poetry has also found a home in publications like Jerry Jazz Musician and The Fictional Café. Beyond his writing, he is an active participant in the global literary community, having read his work and attended seminars in diverse countries such as South Korea, India, the United States, Thailand, Cambodia, and his native Nepal.

www.ingramcontent.com/pod-product-compliance
Lightning Source LLC
LaVergne TN
LVHW092232080526
838199LV00104B/102